INSPIRE

WALKER SCOBELL

BY MARY BLECKWEHL

AMICUS LEARNING

Inspire is published by
Amicus Learning, an imprint of Amicus
P.O. Box 227
Mankato, MN 56002
www.amicuspublishing.us

Editor: Ana Brauer
Series Designer: Kathleen Petelinsek
Book Designer and Photo Researcher: Emily Dietz

Library of Congress Cataloging-in-Publication Data
Names: Bleckwehl, Mary E. author
Title: Walker Scobell / Mary Bleckwehl.
Description: Mankato, MN : Amicus Learning, 2026. | Series: Inspire | Includes bibliographical references and index. |Audience: Ages 5–9 | Audience: Grades 2–3 | Summary: "Lights, camera, action! This engaging biography explores how child actor Walker Scobell rose to fame in *The Adam Project* and *Percy Jackson and the Olympians*. Includes table of contents, glossary, further resources, and index"— Provided by publisher.
Identifiers: LCCN 2025011934 (print) | LCCN 2025011935 (ebook) | ISBN 9798892008662 library binding | ISBN 9798892009324 paperback | ISBN 9798892009980 ebook
Subjects: LCSH: Scobell, Walker—Juvenile literature | Motion picture actors and actresses—United States—Biography—Juvenile literature | LCGFT: Biographies Classification: LCC PN2287. S34125 B54 2026 (print) | LCC PN2287.S34125 (ebook) | DDC 791.4502/8092 [B]—dc23/eng/20250527
LC record available at https://lccn.loc.gov/2025011934
LC ebook record available at https://lccn.loc.gov/2025011935

Photo Credits: Alamy Stock Photo/ATStockFoto, 12, Doug Peters, cover, Skydance Productions / Album, 9, Walt Disney Studios/FlixPix, 5, 13; Getty Images/Corey Nickols, 19, Dia Dipasupil, 6, Jon Kopaloff, 16, Michael Kovac, 20; IMAGO/Capital Pictures, 14, Everett Collection, 10–11; Shutterstock/New Africa, 18, ScofieldZa, 15, Soho A Studio, 7

Printed in the United States of America

Table of Contents

Action Star

A boy jumps onto the head of a monster. It is part-man and part-bull. The boy rips the horn off. He uses it to kill the monster. They are on a **fantasy** TV show set. The monster is fake. But the boy is real. He's Walker Scobell, an American actor.

REAL VS. FAKE

Scobell's hardest scene in *Percy Jackson and the Olympians* (2023) was fighting a fake bull in the dark.

Walker Scobell is known for playing Percy Jackson in the Disney+ series.

Scobell knew from a young age that he wanted to be an actor.

Born to Act

Scobell first acted at age 10. He starred in *Mary Poppins* at his school. After a trip to California, he knew he wanted to be an actor. He joined an acting workshop. Then he signed with an **agent**.

ON THE MOVE!

Scobell's father was in the military. His family moved nine times due to his father's job.

Scobell's first movie was the sci-fi adventure *The Adam Project* (2022).

Breakout Year

At 13, Scobell landed his first big screen role. He costarred with Ryan Reynolds in the Netflix movie *The Adam Project* (2022). There were 376 kids who tried out for the part. Scobell practiced talking like Reynolds. This helped him get the role.

DID YOU KNOW?
Scobell played a younger version of Reynolds's character in *The Adam Project*.

A Bright Young Star

A second movie role came Scobell's way in 2022. He starred as Charlie in the movie *Secret Headquarters*. His character finds a superhero hiding under his home. One **critic** said Scobell's acting was good and stole the show.

Percy Jackson

Since 2023, Scobell's fans know him as 'Percy Jackson.' It's the lead role in the Disney+ series *Percy Jackson and The Olympians.* He plays a **demigod** with superpowers. Scobell was happy to get this role. He was nervous, too.

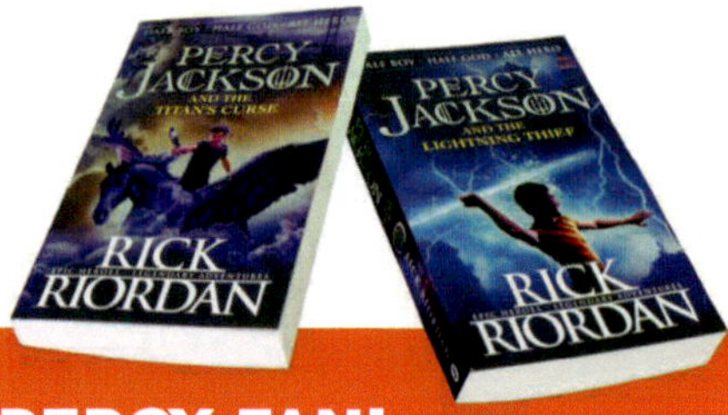

A PERCY FAN!

Scobell started reading the *Percy Jackson* books in third grade. He read all five books seven times.

Scobell plays Percy Jackson, the son of the sea god Poseidon.

Scobell always dreamed of playing Percy Jackson. His dream came true.

A Dream Role

Scobell did many of his own stunts as Percy. He learned to sword fight. The actor spent a lot of time wet. He wore shoes and clothes for underwater scenes. It was challenging. But it was his dream role.

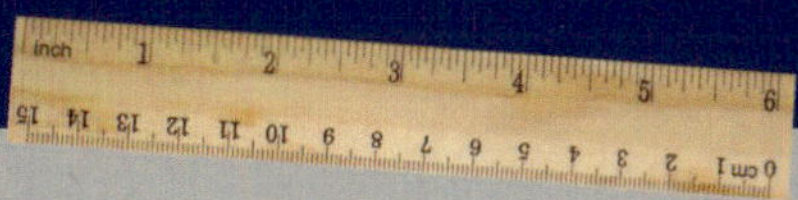

GROWTH SPURT!
Scobell grew 6 inches (15 centimeters) in nine months while filming *Percy Jackson.*

Scobell attended the 2024 Kids' Choice Awards.

Awarded

Percy Jackson was a huge hit. So was Scobell. Kids' Choice Awards gave him the "blimp" award for his role. It was for favorite male TV star in 2024. His hard work paid off.

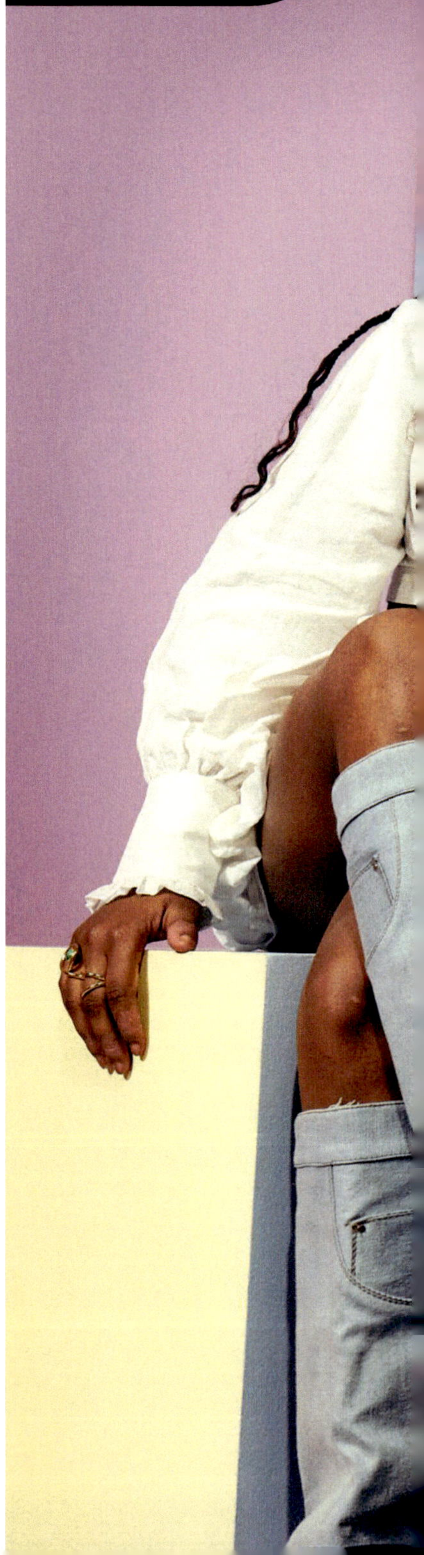

Scobell poses with his *Percy Jackson* costars, Leah Sava Jeffries and Aryan Simhadri.

Feeling Lucky

Scobell feels lucky for his life. He wanted to be an actor, and he is! His parents supported his work. Costars gave him acting tips. He made friends on set. He even learned to scuba dive while acting.

DID YOU KNOW?
Scobell loves extreme sports. He likes **parkour**, skiing, skateboarding, and snowboarding.

Scobell is excited about his future roles and new adventures in acting.

The Next Great Thing

The message in *Percy Jackson* is clear. There's a place for everyone. Scobell has found his. What's next? Will he star as a superhero? He'd like that. He wants to do more of his own stunts. One thing is for sure. Walker Scobell is looking at a long acting career.

SUPER STATS

WALKER SCOBELL

Birthday: January 5, 2009

Birthplace: Virginia Beach, Virginia

Hometown: Fairview, Pennsylvania

Major TV Roles: *Percy Jackson and the Olympians* (2023)

Major Film Roles: *The Adam Project* (2022), *Secret Headquarters* (2022)

AWARDS

Kids' Choice Awards: 2024

Rising Star Award: 2025

GLOSSARY

agent A person who helps actors find work.

critic A person who says what they like and don't like about a performance.

demigod A being in mythology who is part god and part human.

fantasy A story set in an unreal world often with superhuman characters and monsters.

parkour The sport of moving fast through an area by running, jumping, and climbing.

READ MORE

Grack, Rachel. **Curious About Netflix.** Mankato, MN: Amicus Learning, 2026.

Waxman, Laura Hamilton. **Cool Kids Actors.** Minneapolis, MN: Lerner Publications, 2020.

ON THE WEB

Kiddle: Percy Jackson facts for Kids
https://kids.kiddle.co/Percy_Jackson

20 Little-Known Facts About Walker Scobell from Percy Jackson
https://www.youtube.com/watch?v=esYacxOWFRM

Every effort has been made to ensure that these websites are appropriate for children. However, because of the nature of the Internet, it is impossible to guarantee that these sites will remain active indefinitely or that their contents will not be altered.

INDEX

About the Author

Mary Bleckwehl is a children's author who loves cookie dough and talking to kids. She is happiest when she is biking and exploring new places. Mary lives in Minnesota with her husband and monster dog. Check out her books at marybleckwehl.com.